ORPHAN TRAINS

TAKING THE RAILS TO A NEW LIFE

Rebecca Langston-George

Consultant:
Shaley George
Curator, National Orphan Train Complex

Capstone Young Readers
a capstone imprint

Capstone Young Readers are published by Capstone Press, 1710 Roe Crest Drive, North Mankato, MN 56003
www.capstoneyoungreaders.com

Library of Congress Catologing-in-Publication Data
Names: Langston-George, Rebecca, author.
Title: Orphan trains : taking the rails to a new life / by Rebecca
    Langston-George.
Description: North Mankato, Minnesota : Capstone Press, [2017] | Series:
    Encounter: narrative nonfiction stories | Includes bibliographical
    references and index. | Audience: Ages 8-14.
Identifiers: LCCN 2015041585| ISBN 9781491485514 (library binding) |
    ISBN 9781623706302 (paperback) | ISBN
    9781491485538 (ebook pdf)
Subjects: LCSH: Orphan trains--History--Juvenile literature. |
    Orphans--United States--History-Juvenile literature. |
Orphans--United
    States--Biography--Juvenile literature.
Classification: LCC HV985 .L37 2017 | DDC 362.7340973--dc23
LC record available at http://lccn.loc.gov/2015041585

Editorial Credits
Michelle Bisson, editor; Sarah Bennett, designer; Wanda Winch, media researcher;
Laura Manthe, production specialist

Image Credits
Collection of the New-York Historical Society, Children's Aid Society Collection, cover (top), 23-27, 52, 68; Courtesy of author Rebecca Langston-George, 128; Courtesy of Stanley Cornell, 12, 17; Family of Arthur Field Smith, 93; Family of Robert J. Hunt Hume, (NOTC), 65; Family of Ruth Jensen Hickok, 58; Kansas State Historical Society, back cover, 6-7; Library of Congress: Prints and Photographs Division, 36-37, 42, 70-71, 74; National Orphan Train Complex (NOTC), 20, 31, 47, 77, 79, 87; Shutterstock: Gayvoronskaya_Yana, 4-5, 8, 18, 28, 38, 48, 60, 72, 80, 88, 96, 108, igorsky, cover (bottom), Neil Roy Johnson, 116-117, Roberto Castillo, design elements

Printed in China.
009493F16

*To the children who rode the rails,
and for their children and
children's children.*

CONTENTS

There are places enough with good families in Michigan, Illinois, Iowa, and Wisconsin, to give every poor boy and girl in New York a permanent home. The only difficulty is to bring the children to the homes.

— E. P. Smith

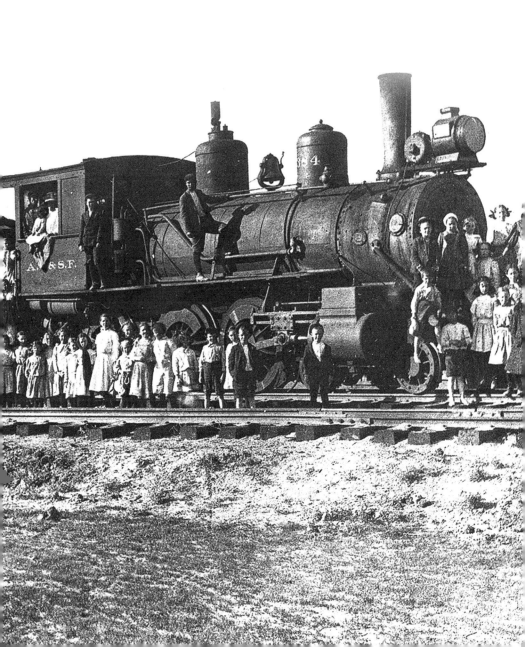

CHAPTER ONE

CLUTCHING HIS BROTHER'S HAND

Stanley Cornell

The December cold seeped through the train compartment. Dozens of children huddled together for warmth in the icy night. Sleeping bodies leaned stacked against one another on the seats. Others sprawled in tangled heaps across the wooden train floor. Below them the train wheels sped down the tracks. Six-year-old Stanley Cornell burrowed deeper under his single blanket. Curled up beside him on the floor was his younger brother, Victor.

Stanley thought again of Mama, Daddy, and baby Eloise. He hadn't seen them for two years. But he could still picture the scene around Mama's bed as if it had happened yesterday. Eloise had just been born. Mama was sick. Four-year-old Stanley stood next to Mama's bed. She was crying. She must have known she was dying when she took Stanley's hand.

In ragged breaths Mama whispered, "Be good to Daddy." And that was all.

Stanley never saw Mama again. He tried to be good to Daddy Floyd. But Daddy Floyd wasn't well either. He'd been a soldier in World War I. Doctors said he had shell-shock. And he'd been hurt by nerve gas. His body hurt and his mind was often cloudy. Daddy Floyd wasn't well enough to work a steady job. With Mama gone he couldn't take care of the three of them.

Not long after Mama died, the lady in the big black car showed up. She handed Stanley and Victor each a piece of candy. She scooped Eloise up in her arms. "I'll have to take the children," she said.

Stanley, Victor, and Eloise were put in the big black car. As the car drove off, Stanley turned to look out the car's back window. Daddy Floyd stood on the porch, one hand clinging to the rail. With his other hand Daddy Floyd took a handkerchief from his pocket. He wiped the tears streaming down his face.

Daddy Floyd stood on the porch, one hand clinging to the rail. With his other hand Daddy Floyd took a handkerchief from his pocket. He wiped the tears streaming down his face.

The big black car took them to an orphanage run by the Children's Aid Society of New York. Baby Eloise was quickly adopted by their aunt. But with five children of her own already, the aunt had no room for Stanley and Victor. They would have to stay at the orphanage.

Stanley, six (left), and his brother, Victor, age four, were all alone in the world—except for one another.

Orphanage life was hard for Stanley and Victor. The older kids picked on youngsters like them, stealing their food. But fighting back wasn't a good idea. Breaking a rule meant being beaten.

Then in December of 1927 Stanley and Victor were told they'd be riding the train. The train west meant a possible new home. Agents from the orphanage herded more than a hundred children aboard the train. The night before, they'd all had baths. Everyone was given clean new clothes. They had to look sharp so they'd be picked by a new family.

The train rattled down the tracks for days. First they went down the length of the East Coast. Then they took a turn west, crossing Mississippi and Louisiana. Whenever the train stopped, all the children climbed off. They brushed themselves off, smoothed their clothes, and lined up outside the train. The small ones stood on top of wooden crates. People came by to look them over. Many asked questions. A few peered inside their mouths to inspect their teeth. Sometimes people thumped the children's muscles to see how strong they were.

They couldn't be separated. He wouldn't let that happen. He'd lost Mama, Daddy Floyd, and Eloise. No one would take Victor from him.

Like cattle, Stanley thought. *Much like farmers would do at an auction.* He held onto Victor's hand tightly. They couldn't be separated. He wouldn't let that happen. He'd lost Mama, Daddy Floyd, and Eloise. No one would take Victor from him.

When the looking was over, the unwanted orphans returned to the train. At every stop there were fewer children loaded back on the train. As the train pulled away toward the next station, Stanley and the other orphans watched out the windows as the chosen ones walked off with new families.

The week before Christmas the train arrived at Wellington, Texas. It was evening and a blinding snow raged around them. Only a handful of children were left on the train, and Stanley and Victor were the only boys left. They had plenty of room to spread out on the seats. But when the train stopped they were hurried through the dark night with snow pelting their faces. Soon they were inside the warm lobby of the Wellington Hotel. Stanley grabbed his brother's hand and held it tightly. A few people looked the remaining children over.

What if they weren't picked? The train route was almost finished. Would they have to go back to the orphanage? Stanley and his brother had already had one bad experience six months earlier. He and Victor had been placed with a couple in Coffeyville, Kansas. But without explaining why, the couple had sent Stanley and Victor back to the orphanage after only a few months. Being unwanted left an empty pit inside Stanley. And the sting of sadness had haunted him ever since.

"Do you like horses?" a man asked. He knelt down near Stanley and added, "How about cows, chickens, and pigs?"

Stanley nodded. His eyes slid over to Victor. Stanley pulled him closer. They belonged together and he wanted the man to know that.

The farmer smiled and went off to talk to one of the agents. Stanley heard them talking. The farmer only needed one boy. Stanley's heart sank.

The farmer smiled and went off to talk to one of the agents. Stanley heard them talking. The farmer only needed one boy. Stanley's heart sank.

When the farmer, J. L. Deger, returned and motioned for Stanley to come with him, Stanley began to cry. He clung to Victor and wouldn't move.

The farmer thought of his wife and daughters back in their home by the wood-burning stove. He hadn't told them he planned to bring even one boy home. But he knew what he had to do. Once again he talked to the agent. When he returned he led both Stanley and Victor out to his brand new Model T car. He handed them a bag of jelly beans to share. Then he bundled them up in blankets for the ride home. Their new home.

Stanley and his brother, Victor (left), found a good home on a farm—most importantly, they found a home together!

CHAPTER TWO

MISSIONARY TO "STREET RATS"

Stanley and Victor ended up in a loving home in 1927. Their happy ending can be traced back to 1853 when a young minister living in New York decided to take action. Charles Loring Brace knew thousands of children just like Stanley. Sadly, stories of homeless children were common in the 1800s and early 1900s. Many children in big cities like New York were orphaned. Others were abandoned or given up by parents like Daddy Floyd who could no longer take care of them.

As tens of thousands of immigrants poured into cities like New York, the living conditions became crowded. Poor sanitation and hygiene led to diseases such as typhus and cholera. Vaccines and most modern medicines were not yet available,

Charles Loring Brace

so the sick often died rather than being cured. The high death rate among young adults left many children orphaned.

In the 1850s more than 30,000 children lived alone on New York City's streets.

Orphanages, also called asylums, overflowed with homeless children. The streets in poor, crowded areas like the Five Points District of New York were filled with homeless children struggling to survive. Called "street rats," they sold newspapers or apples, shined shoes, and picked through the trash for rags to sell. Many also picked people's pockets to survive. In the 1850s more than 30,000 children lived alone on New York City's streets.

With no shelter for warmth, winter was especially difficult for these children. Brace wrote, "Two little newsboys slept one winter in the iron tube of the bridge at Harlem; two others made their bed in a burned-out safe in Wall Street. Sometimes they ensconced themselves in the cabin of a ferry-boat, and thus spent the night. Old boilers, barges, steps, and, above all, steam-gratings were their favorite beds."

Churches and civic organizations began missions and charities to help the poor in areas such as Five Points. Most of these charities helped adults. But the young Reverend Brace in the Five Points area made it his mission to serve the children.

Brace wrote his father in 1852, "I want to raise up the outcast and homeless, to go down among those who have no friend or helper, and do something for them…"

Brace did "do something" for the city's orphans. He founded the Children's Aid Society in 1853. Several other ministers and city leaders joined his cause. Their first task was to raise money to run the society. Brace printed ads describing the work that the society would do. He planned to open schools, lodging houses, and reading rooms. The society would also train children for jobs. In addition, he had a new idea to help the orphaned children. He wanted to send them out of the city to live and work on farms.

Charles knew that French orphanages were "placing out" babies in families. People in France were paid to care for the infants in their own homes. He liked the idea of children living within a family instead of an institution. So the Children's Aid Society's goals became to give children a family life, education, and work training.

Once they raised the funds to do so, the society opened a lodging house for newsboys. These boys were proud of their independence. So Brace decided to "give them nothing without payment, but at the same time to offer them much more for their money than they could get anywhere else." One night at the lodge cost six cents and included a bath. Dinner was four cents. The Newsboys' Lodging also started a savings bank where the boys could deposit their coins and earn interest.

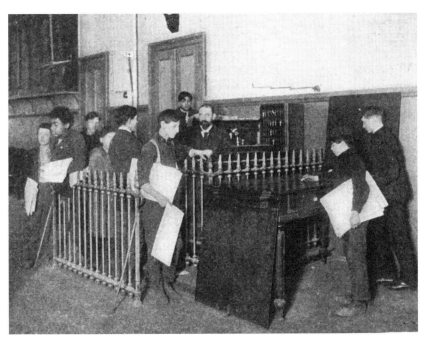

The newsboys deposited their earnings in their own savings bank.

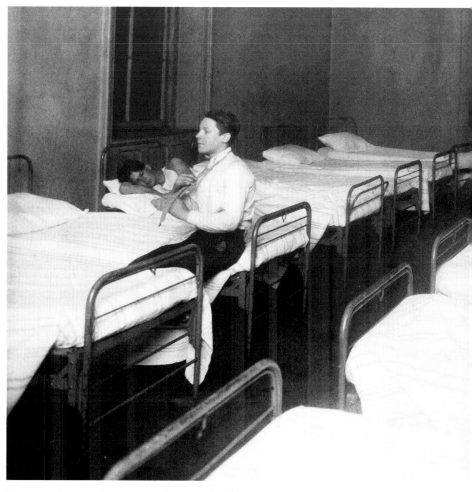

The newsboys got a warm bath and a bed for six cents a night.

To serve homeless girls, the society opened an industrial school for girls. Here girls could learn to sew, cook, and clean. With these skills they could find paying work as seamstresses or maids.

The Newsboys' Lodging House and Industrial School for Girls helped many children in the city. But

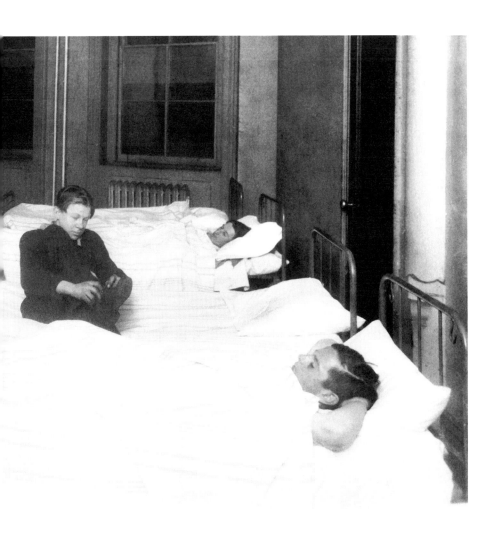

Brace believed children would be better off in the country. Farmers needed help planting and taking care of animals. Orphaned and neglected children needed a family. Brace decided the best way to connect the two was by train.

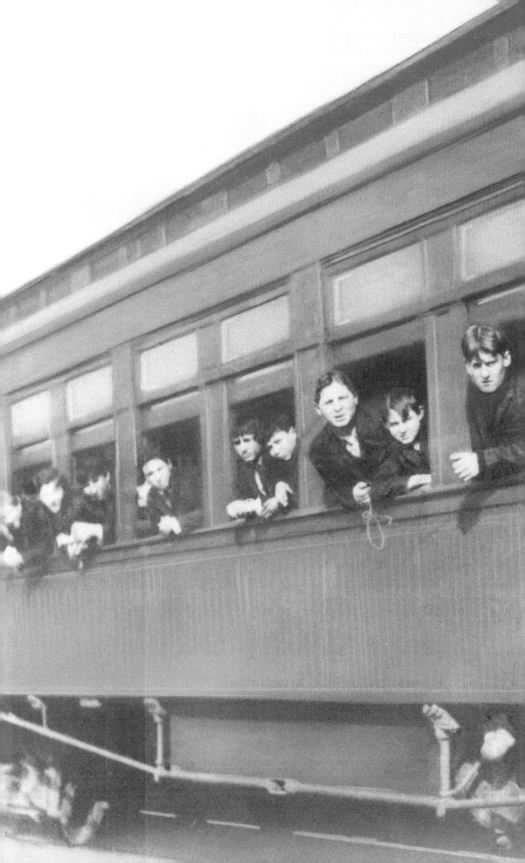

On that first trip [in 1854] all but nine children found a place. ... Those nine later boarded the train once more and went to Chicago and Iowa City to find homes.

THREE CHEERS FOR MICHIGAN, THE FIRST ORPHAN TRAIN

On the evening of September 28, 1854, Charles Loring Brace sent the first group of 37 orphans out to find new homes in the west. To get to Dowagiac, Michigan, they didn't start out on a train. Instead, they climbed up the gangplank of the riverboat *Isaac Newton* in New York. Each of them had received new clothes for the trip. They'd also visited a shoe shop and been fitted with new shoes. One little boy nicknamed Little Jack hardly knew how to put his on. He hadn't owned a pair of shoes in three winters.

In high spirits, the children sang as they boarded the ship. Each one clutched a steerage ticket. Steerage was the cheapest way to ride. It was the lowest deck, where animals were kept. Fleas and lice infested the rough sleeping mats where steerage passengers slept. But when the ship's captain heard the children singing he invited them to come meet him. Touched by their stories, he offered them better beds.

The captain wasn't the only one fascinated by the orphan children. Although Brace's plan had been to find the children homes in Dowagiac, some of the passengers had other ideas. A woman from Rochester, New York, begged to take one boy. A shop owner from Illinois took another boy, nicknamed Liverpool.

At six the next morning the ship docked in Albany, New York. The children, aged six to fifteen, got off the boat with the Children's Aid Society (C.A.S.) agent E. P. Smith. Nine more children were waiting at the train depot with another C.A.S. agent to join them.

The train station was flooded with passengers. Mr. Smith tried to talk the train's conductor into

Homes For Children
═══ WANTED ═══

A Company of Homeless Children from the East Will Arrive at

McPherson, Friday, September 15.

These children are of various ages and of both sexes, having been thrown friendless upon the world. They come under the auspices of the Children's Aid Society, of New York. They are well disciplined, having come from various orphanages. The citizens of this community are asked to assist the agent in finding good homes for them. Persons taking these children must be recommended by the local committee. They must treat the children in every way as members of the family, sending them to school, church, Sabbath school and properly clothe them until they are 18 years old. Protestant children placed in Protestant homes and Catholic children in Catholic homes. The following well known citizens have agreed to act as a local committee to aid the agents in securing homes:

| Dr. Heaston | H. A. Rowland | C. W. Bachelor |
| F. A. Vaniman | W. J. Krehbiel | K. Sorensen |

Applications must be made to and endorsed by the local committee.

An address will be given by the agents. Come and see the children and hear the address. Distribution will take place at

Opera House, Friday, September 15
at 10:00 a. m. and 2:00 p. m.

Before each stop on the train line, flyers were posted to let interested families know when the orphans would arrive.

giving the orphans their own car. He agreed. But when the doors opened a mass of unruly people rushed in. So, the orphans had to be separated into several different cars. Still, they made the best of it. They ate crackers and gingerbread and sang.

Although the crowded conditions didn't dampen their spirits, the children were in for a surprise when the sun set. The conductor announced, "Passengers must furnish their own lights." Most of them had never had two pennies to rub together, much less owned a kerosene lantern or candles. So it was a long, dark night.

When the sun rose the next morning the train was passing through the New York countryside.

Each new sight caused the children to cry out in delight. But the best sight of all was a pumpkin patch full of yellow-orange globes. "Oh! Oh! Look at them!"

"What's that, mister?" asked one. "A cornfield?" Many of the children oohed and aahed, having never been out of the city.

"Look at them cows!" yelled another.

Apple orchards and more cornfields sped by the windows. Each new sight caused the children to cry out in delight. But the best sight of all was a pumpkin patch full of yellow-orange globes. "Oh! Oh! Look at them!"

They were still several states away from Michigan. But everyone agreed Michigan would be full of good things to eat. "Won't we have nice things to eat!"

"Hip! Hip, boys! Three cheers for Michigan!"

It took one more boat ride and another train ride before they reached Michigan at 3:00 a.m. on Sunday. Exhausted, many of the children lay down on the railway platform to sleep.

When the sun rose, the agent, Mr. Smith, rounded up all the children and took them to breakfast at a nearby restaurant. After washing up, they walked to the Presbyterian Church. The children gathered acorns and flowers on the way. One little girl stuck a corn leaf in Mr. Smith's buttonhole. "It's a nosegay," she said.

People from all over had come to see the orphan children. Smith lined up the children and they sang.

"Come, ye sinners, poor and needy,

Weak and wounded, sick and sore;

Jesus ready stands to save you,

Full of pity, love and power."

Several people had to pull handkerchiefs out to wipe away tears. The minister preached and announced that Mr. Smith would be back in the afternoon with another sermon. Mr. Smith said that anyone interested in taking home one of the children should come and see him.

The next day Mr. Smith talked to the families wanting to take home a child. He asked local pastors and the justice of the peace if they recommended these families. He also talked to the children to see if they wanted to go with them. Fifteen children were placed that day. The Children's Aid Society said "the children are not indentured, (bound to serve by a contract) but are free to leave, if ill-treated or dissatisfied; and the farmers can dismiss them if they find them useless or otherwise unsuitable." Although the children were free to leave, they were expected to work. So the adults who chose them were usually called "employers" rather than parents in the early years of the orphan trains.

On that first trip all but nine children found a place in Dowagiac. Those nine later boarded the train once more and went to Chicago and Iowa City to find homes.

Mr. Smith said, "... The first experiment of sending children West is a very happy one, and I am sure there are places enough with good families in Michigan, Illinois, Iowa and Wisconsin, to give every poor boy and girl in New York a permanent home. The only difficulty is to bring the children to the homes."

The train's next stop was … Noblesville, Indiana. As [the children] ate, curious people came by to look them over. "It was the most motley crowd of youngsters I ever did see," said Judge John Green.

CHAPTER FOUR

FROM NEWSBOY TO NEWS MAKER

Andrew Burke

On May 15, 1850, Andrew Horace Burke took his first breaths. At the same time his mother, Mary Burke, drew her last breath on this earth. She died while giving birth to him. His father, John, was left with a tiny baby and a broken heart.

John Burke worked all day in a factory. He barely earned enough money to survive. There were no relatives to help care for baby Andrew. So neighbors in the tenement where John Burke lived took turns watching the baby.

In 1854, when Andrew was just four years old, his father died. Andrew Burke was now completely alone in the world. The neighbors who had babysat him got together to discuss his future. Poor and barely able to feed their own families, none of the neighbors could take Andrew in. One of them delivered Andrew to the orphanage at Randall's Island.

A year later, at the age of five, Andrew Horace Burke began to make his own living on the tough streets of New York.

A year later, at the age of five, Andrew Horace Burke began to make his own living on the tough streets of New York. He got a job with the *New York Tribune* newspaper as a newsboy. Before dawn each day he used the money he earned the previous day to buy a stack of papers as big as he could carry. He paid three cents for every two copies of the *Tribune*.

The newspaper assigned him a street corner to sell the papers.

Andrew couldn't read, so the other newsboys taught him how to sound out the words in the top stories. Yelling out headlines like "James Buchanan Elected President," Andrew charged two cents for each paper sold. Through snow, rain, and howling wind Andrew stayed on his corner until all his papers were sold. He couldn't return unsold papers so he had to work hard. Otherwise he would lose money.

When the morning papers were sold Andrew carefully pocketed the coins he made on each sale. He spent part of his earnings on lunch. In the afternoon he returned to the newspaper to buy copies of the afternoon edition. Then he headed back to his corner to sell papers again. He did this seven days a week.

Most days he earned between twenty-five to fifty cents from selling newspapers. If there was an important news story that day he might earn a little more. Most of his money went toward buying papers to sell. He also spent money to stay at the Newsboys'

Newsboys sell papers on the Brooklyn Bridge in 1908.

Lodging. Every day he spent four cents for dinner in the dining room on the first floor. Later, tired from a long day's work, he paid six cents for a warm place to sleep. Then he trudged upstairs to one of the iron bunk beds.

The Newsboys' Lodging also had a reading room. The newsboys could read the Bible, newspapers, and books in the evening. Slowly Andrew began to learn how to read the newspapers that he sold. He grew bigger and could carry more newspapers to sell. This earned him a few extra pennies. Although he worked hard, he rarely had extra money for warm clothes or shoes.

Tales of the orphans traveling west had made their way to the Newsboys' Lodging. One night one of the boys stood upon a chair and gave a speech as a joke.

"Boys, (gentlemen), chummies: (Perhaps) you'd like to hear (something) about the West, the great West, you know, where so many of our old friends are settled

When Andrew Burke got the chance to go west he gladly took it. He was nine years old when he boarded the train in August of 1859. Another newsboy took over Andrew's old corner. Peddling the newspapers, the new boy called out the *Tribune* headlines, which often included stories of orphans heading west.

"Yesterday afternoon Mr. C. C. Tracy left this city

for the West, with another company of little ones

from the Children's Aid Society. … Who knows what

dangers they may have escaped by their fortunate

adoption by the Children's Aid Society? … The

company was comfortably and neatly fitted out for their expedition. Of the boys, several had been on the verge of extreme poverty and exposed to ... evils of temptation and crime. They rejoiced much in their fortunate rescue."

Reverend Brace gave Andrew and the other 26 children headed west a Bible inscribed with their names. The train ride was long and Andrew dreaded the waiting and wondering whether he'd be picked. But he discovered another rider he knew from the Randall's Island orphanage. John Brady was a tough street kid who had given himself two tattoos before his tenth birthday. John and Andrew quickly became best friends. John and Andrew laughed and talked the miles away. Both were good-looking youngsters, quick-witted and quick to smile.

The train trip took a week. On the last day the train made a stop in Tipton, Indiana. A man in a dark suit and hat, carrying a cane, boarded the train. He stood by the door to the orphan's train car and watched them.

The train's next stop was a few miles down the tracks in Noblesville, Indiana. The C.A.S. agent, Mr. Friedgen, took the children to lunch at Aunt Jenny Fergusson's hotel. As they ate, curious people came by to look them over. The mysterious man with the cane watched Andrew and John carefully as they ate. "It was the most motley crowd of youngsters I ever did see," the man said.

Later, the children walked to the local church. There, the townspeople were waiting to choose which children to take home. It turned out the mysterious man, a local judge named John Green, had decided to adopt an orphan boy. Figuring the children would be on their best behavior at the church, he had decided to see for himself what they were really like. That's why he watched them on the train and at lunch. "I decided to take John Brady home with me because I considered him the homeliest, toughest, most unpromising boy in the whole lot. I had a curious desire to see what could be made of such a specimen of humanity."

Several people offered to take Andrew home. He chose to go home with Mr. D. W. Butler, a local farmer, because he looked gentle.

In his letters to the Children's Aid Society Andrew said the Butlers were good to him. He was grateful for the opportunity to go west. He lived with three different families before becoming an adult. As a teen he served as a drummer boy with the 75th Indiana Regiment during the Civil War.

The newsboy who learned to read by studying headlines later worked for the Evansville *Courier* newspaper. But it wouldn't be long before Andrew Burke became big news himself. His name was destined to appear in lots of newspaper headlines.

Andrew Burke

CHAPTER FIVE

A BABY DOLL OF HER OWN

Agnes Ruth Anderson Hickok

Agnes Herlin was too young to remember the day Daddy walked out. He left Mama, Agnes, and baby Evelyn and never returned. Mama had no way to pay the rent. She had to find a job. With a baby and a toddler to take care of, it wasn't easy to find work. Making it even more difficult, Mama only spoke Norwegian. She had emigrated from Norway so recently she hadn't learned English.

Finally, Mama was lucky enough to find work as a live-in housekeeper. Even luckier, the job came with a bedroom to live in. The family also allowed Mama to bring three-month-old baby Evelyn with her. But Agnes wasn't so lucky. The family wouldn't let Mama bring 22-month-old Agnes to her new job.

In 1914 Mama took Agnes to the New York Foundling Hospital. Although it was called a hospital, the big stone building was actually an orphanage. At first Mama visited Agnes every week. Mama brought hugs, kisses, and promises that they'd be together again soon.

When Agnes was four, Mama came for her weekly visit. But Mama wasn't the same as usual. "Don't touch me," Mama said. "I'm sick." Agnes cried. She reached out for Mama but wasn't allowed to touch her. Mama never visited again.

Every night Agnes knelt on the cold, hard floor beside her white iron bed. She clasped her hands together and prayed as the nuns had taught her. But inside she felt empty. When she lay down to sleep she dreamed of a crying baby. Somewhere out there a baby was crying for her.

There was never enough food. … She learned to hold her plate next to her and shield it with her arms. She ate quickly, shoveling in as much as she could before someone stole it.

Tears were everywhere at the orphanage. There was never enough food. Older children snatched what little food Agnes was given. She learned to hold her plate next to her and shield it with her arms. She ate quickly, shoveling in as much as she could before someone stole it.

Her clothes had belonged to someone else before her. They were worn and patched. When she outgrew them they'd go to someone else. The wooden toys on the orphanage shelves were old and broken. They were for all the children. Agnes did not have a single thing to call her own.

In 1917 when Agnes was five someone pinned a silk ribbon with her name on it to her coat. C.A.S. agent Clara Comstock led Agnes and 40 other children to the train station.

Five-year-old Agnes was confused by the train ride. Each time the train stopped the children got off. People looked at them. Then they got back on the train. But some children didn't get back on.

Between 1911 and 1928 C.A.S. agent Clara Comstock (right) made 74 train trips to place orphans with families.

Agnes cried for them. "Don't worry," another orphan told her. "They landed."

The train ride took many days. Agnes was hungry. She was always hungry. There was nothing to eat but mustard sandwiches. She didn't like the spicy yellow mustard. But she didn't like being hungry either. So she ate the mustard sandwiches and didn't complain.

When the conductor came into the orphan's train car with a basket of apples Agnes grew excited. Apples! Yummy! But when he handed her an apple it was full of worms. Agnes frowned. The only thing worse than a mustard sandwich was a wormy apple.

The conductor pulled the window down. "Throw it!" he said.

Agnes looked down at her apple. What if there were no more mustard sandwiches?

The conductor picked a wormy apple from the basket and hurled it out the window. "See?" he said. "The seeds inside the apple will grow apple trees next to the train tracks."

Agnes laughed. She threw her apple with all her might and reached for another.

When the train stopped at Forest City, Iowa, Agnes slipped her feet back into her too-tight shoes. She climbed off the train and followed agent Comstock and the other children to a church. She was tired and her feet hurt. As the children lined up for people to look them over they each received a cookie. It was much better than a mustard sandwich but Agnes was still hungry.

Men and women walked up and down the line looking at the children. Some of them asked questions but Agnes couldn't understand everything they said. She was still learning English.

Two couples asked to take Agnes home. Later that day agent Comstock took Agnes to the older couple's home. "This nice lady will be your mother," she said.

When Miss Comstock left Agnes became scared. She began to cry.

"Stop that crying!" the old woman said. She grabbed Agnes by the shoulders and shook her. Frightened, tired, and hungry, Agnes just cried more.

Slap! The blow stung Agnes's cheek. She grew more afraid and cried even harder.

The old woman angrily rained more blows down on tiny Agnes's back and legs. "Stop that crying right now!" But Agnes couldn't stop.

When Agnes continued to sob the woman threw her in the cold, dark cellar. With a click of the lock five-year-old Agnes was trapped.

"If you don't stop that crying you'll get no supper." When Agnes continued to sob the woman threw her in the cold, dark cellar. With a click of the lock, five-year-old Agnes was trapped.

Agnes clung to the top stair leading to the cellar door. The air was dank and musty. In the dark she couldn't see what was below. Why had Miss Comstock left her here? Exhausted, Agnes laid her cheek against the cold step and cried herself to sleep.

The next morning Agnes woke up to the sound of a ringing doorbell. When her eyes adjusted to the light she realized she was lying on the kitchen floor. The old woman must have pulled her out of the cellar.

Agent Comstock stood over Agnes. She had come to check on her. Tears welled up in Agnes's eyes once more. She grabbed Miss Comstock's legs and wouldn't let go.

"This isn't going to work out," Miss Comstock said to the old woman. "Please get Agnes's things."

Miss Comstock walked Agnes to a café and gave her a glass of milk. Agnes hadn't had anything to eat or drink since yesterday's cookie. The cold glass of milk soothed her throat, sore from all the crying.

Afterward Miss Comstock and Agnes walked to a big white house surrounded by lots of green trees.

Miss Comstock knocked on the door. It was opened by the other couple who had wanted Agnes the day before at the church. Ted and Nattie Jensen owned a wagon business.

Agnes grabbed Miss Comstock once more. "I don't want to sleep in a cellar where it's black and smelly!"

Agnes hugged the plate to her stomach and held her arms over it. She didn't want anyone to take her food. Mrs. Jensen smiled and spooned more food on Agnes's plate.

But Agnes never had to sleep in a cellar again. The Jensens loved her and took good care of her. When Mrs. Jensen served dinner, Agnes hugged the plate to her stomach and held her arms over it. She didn't want anyone to take her food. Mrs. Jensen smiled and spooned more food on Agnes's plate.

"Is it all mine?" Agnes asked. Mrs. Jensen nodded. Slowly Agnes moved her arms.

The Jensens had two sons and two spinster aunts who lived with them. One aunt was named Agnes. Soon it became confusing having two people named Agnes living in the house. Agnes and the Jensens decided she needed a new name. They chose the name Ruth.

Agnes was renamed Ruth. She grew up in a happy home but missed her sister, Evelyn.

For the first time in her life Ruth had new things that belonged just to her. Mrs. Jensen and the aunts sewed new clothes for Ruth. For Christmas Ruth got her first toy, a beautiful new doll. She rocked it and sang to it. She whispered promises in her doll's ear. "You'll never sleep in a dark smelly cellar." She loved taking care of her baby doll.

But even a porcelain doll of her very own couldn't fill the emptiness in Ruth's heart. At night she still dreamed of a crying baby. Not a day went by that Ruth didn't feel she was missing something in her life.

CHAPTER SIX

JUST AN ADOPTED BRAT

Robert Hunt had loved music for as long as he could remember. But there was one instrument he hated. The sound of an accordion always made him sad.

His father played the accordion. On the weekends he played at parties and clubs in New York City. He also worked as a driver. But when Robert was born in Greenwich Village in lower New York City at the turn of the century—1900, his father could barely make ends meet. He had a hard time earning enough money to care for Robert and his older sisters, Sadie and Margaret.

Before long Mr. Hunt was out of work and broke. Desperate, Mr. and Mrs. Hunt left their three children with their grandparents. The children stayed together a few months in the old narrow building on a brick road called Christopher Street.

But it wasn't long before Margaret and Sadie were taken to the Five Point House of Industry orphanage in New York City. The family kept baby Robert a little while longer, but eventually he was taken to the orphanage as well.

In September 1904 Robert, aged four, along with his sisters, Sadie, aged six, and 10-year-old Margaret, were sent on the orphan train west.

Margaret and Sadie looked after Robert on the long, bumpy trip. They wiped his sticky hands after he ate raspberry jelly sandwiches. Snuggled together on the seat, they whispered of the good times they'd have together in the country. And they passed the long hours looking out the window at the green and gold fields.

But halfway to Iowa the agents noticed something odd. Many of the 17 children on the train were scratching their heads. The C.A.S. agent checked and found several of them had head lice. With all of them packed closely together in the train car it wouldn't be long before everyone had it.

Snip! Snip! Snip! The C.A.S. agent cut off their hair. Some of the girls cried as their brown or blond locks fell to their feet.

The conductor stopped the train. The itchy children were ordered off. Snip! Snip! Snip! The C.A.S. agent cut off their hair. Some of the girls cried as their brown or blond locks fell to their feet. Embarrassed and worried no family would pick them now, the stubbly-headed orphans climbed back aboard the train.

In Sidney, Iowa, the 17 passengers got off the train. Margaret and Sadie held Robert's hands as they walked to the town's newly built Methodist church. Inside, they lined up at the front as townspeople filled the pews to take a look at them.

Their dreams of good times together in the country quickly evaporated as no one wanted to take all three of them. Tears streamed down their faces as they realized they would be separated.

Mrs. Hutchinson, who had three sons and had always wanted a daughter, chose Sadie. As they were driving home, her new mother gave Sadie a bracelet and some candy. Broken-hearted at leaving her siblings, she said, "I'll give you back the bracelet and the candy if you give me back my sister."

But her sister, Margaret, was chosen by another family. Unlike Sadie's family, who loved her, Margaret's only wanted a free employee. A neighbor described them as "the meanest family you could imagine." Badly abused and overworked, Margaret was eventually removed from that home. She ended up being handed off to one family after another. When the census was taken in 1910, 16-year-old Margaret was listed as a servant in the household. Even as an adult Margaret refused to talk about what happened to her with "the meanest family you could imagine."

Robert's adoptive family did not treat him well, but one saving grace was that he was able to spend time with his older sister, Sadie.

With a stroke of a pen, Robert was given to Guy and Alma Hume. They signed a document like this, which C.A.S. used for most placements.

I, the undersigned _____ hereby agree to provide for _____ now the age of ___ years until the said boy shall reach the age of 18 years according to the following terms and conditions, and with the full understanding that the Society reserves the right to remove the child previous to legal adoption. If at any time the circumstances of the home such as in the judgment of the agent are injurious to the physical, mental or moral well-being of the child. The terms and the conditions for the retention of the boy in my family being as follows: To care for him in sickness and in health, to send him to school during the entire school year until he reaches the age of 16 years; also to have him attend church and Sunday school and to retain him as a member of my family until he reaches the age of 17 years, and thereafter for the final year, until he is 18 years old, to pay the boy monthly wages in addition to his maintenance, the amount thereof to be previously determined after consultation with the Society's local agent and his approval. In case he proves unsatisfactory, I agree to notify the Society, and pending his removal, to keep him a reasonable length of time after such notice has been given. I agree, moreover, to use my best endeavor then and at all times to detain him, should he try to leave me, until the Society can take steps for his removal. I agree to keep him at all times as well supplied with clothing as he was when I received him. It is understood and agreed on my part that after the period of five years following the date of placement has elapsed, the Society cannot be called upon for removal. I agree to write the Society at least once a year, and should I change my address I will notify the Society.

Robert was later legally adopted by Guy and Alma Hume. Their son, who had been the same age as Robert, had recently died. The Humes didn't live far from the Hutchinsons, with whom Sadie had been placed. The two of them were allowed to see each other occasionally.

The Children's Aid Society

HOME FINDING DEPARTMENT

UNITED CHARITIES BUILDING

105 EAST 22D STREET, NEW YORK

REPORT OF A VISIT TO A WARD OF THE SOCIETY

No.		When Placed in Present Home
Name of Child	Present Age	Date Visited
With Whom Placed	Post Office Address	R. F. D. No.
County	State	Distance From Home to School
Name of Most Convenient Railroad Station	Distance to Home	Direction
What is Acreage of Place	Owned or Rented	Occupation of Foster Father

How Many Children Living at Home

Boys	Age	Girls	Age

Number of Persons in Family			Number of Hired Help
Condition of the House as to Cleanliness	Order	Comfort	Appearance of House, Yard, Barn, Etc.
Is the Home Adapted to the Child		Observe Relations Between Child and Foster Parents	
Condition of the Child as to Health	Clothing		Manners
Does Child Sleep Alone in Separate Room		If Not, Where and With Whom	
Is Child Happy	Was Child Seen Alone		Any Bad Habits
Do Foster Parents Direct Reading		What Literature Provided	

(over)

EB-2M-2-25-20   Printing Class. C. A. S.

After each visit to a child who had been placed with a family, the agent filled out a report.

68

Although Robert was grateful to be near Sadie, Robert's life with the Humes wasn't happy. They thought he didn't measure up as a "replacement" for their lost son. Mrs. Hume had a bad temper, which she often took out on Robert. When he displeased her, she yelled, "You're just an adopted brat."

Both of his adopted parents drank heavily. Mr. Hume also abused opium. As a result of the drug abuse, Mr. Hume had to be put in an institution for treatment.

With his parents often drunk or absent, much of the work fell on Robert. Although he was young, he worked hard. His adoptive parents had signed a contract promising to send him to school until he was 16. But Robert had to quit before finishing eighth grade to work full time. At night he read books and taught himself as much as he could.

Despite Robert's difficult circumstances, he was always optimistic. With hard work and determination he made the best of what life gave him. Still, the notes of an accordion made him wish for something long missing in his life: a happy and whole family.

As the train sped by the barren winter countryside, Miss Comstock … coached the children on how to act. "Mind your manners. Smile. Don't be shy," said Clara Comstock.

CHAPTER SEVEN

THREE MOTHERS AND MANY SISTERS

Edith Peterson

The woman bundled three-week-old Edith tighter in her blanket to keep out the February cold. Far from her Norwegian home and recently widowed, the young mother couldn't take care of her newborn. She kissed the baby's pink cheek one last time. Then she tucked tiny Edith inside the bassinet outside the door to the New York Foundling Hospital. Inside the orphanage a bell rang alerting the nuns that another baby had been left.

The bell at the Foundling Hospital had been ringing nearly every day since it opened in 1869. It was founded by Sister Irene and her order, the Sisters of Charity. Sister Irene had heard stories of infants thrown away like garbage. She made it her life's mission to provide a safe shelter for New York's abandoned babies. With an empty apartment building, five dollars, and one crib, she opened the New York Foundling Hospital. Within the first year more than a thousand children were left for Sister Irene and her fellow nuns to care for.

Sister Irene created a safe haven for thousands of abandoned babies.

In February 1912 baby Edith Peterson became the orphanage's newest resident. But she didn't stay long. When she was 22 months old a nun pinned a ribbon with the number 41 to Edith's clothes. She was loaded on the orphan train November 29, 1913.

In Avon, Minnesota, John and Mary Bieganek waited for baby girl 41. They had a letter with the matching number telling them where to meet their new child. Unlike the Children's Aid Society, the Foundling Hospital tried to match its youngest children with families before sending them on the train. Catholic families could write to the agency or ask their priest to write on their behalf and ask for a child. The nuns would try to match the age, hair, and eye color requested.

When the little mail-order orphan climbed down the train steps, she let go of the agent's hand and ran right into her new father's arms. He scooped her up and took Edith home to the Bieganek's already large family. Even though they had many older children, John and Mary Bieganek were eager to take in little

Edith. A curious new toddler was just what Mary Bieganek needed. Edith fit right in on the Bieganek's farm with her many new sisters and brothers. She loved her new Polish family.

But it wasn't long before tragedy struck and Edith was left without a mother once more. Her adopted mother died of cancer when Edith was six. Her bereaved father and older brothers didn't know what to do with her. One brother, Walter, began taking care of her as best he could. He made sure she had clean clothes and went to bed at night.

When her brother Joseph married his sweetheart, Rose, they decided that Edith would live with them. Her adopted father moved to another town. He thought life with Joseph and Rose would be better for Edith because she would have a mother.

It was a very confusing time for eight-year-old Edith. She was told to call her brother "Father" and his new wife "Mother." Her new mother spoke Polish and insisted Edith learn the language too. And for the first time she was enrolled in school.

Edith became the beloved youngest sibling in her adoptive family.

Joseph and Rose began a family right away. They had 13 children and depended on Edith to help raise them. Edith changed diapers, rocked babies, and cleaned house. There was always a new baby or a toddler who needed her. She rarely had a moment to herself. Although she loved Joseph and Rose and all the children she felt like something was missing in her life.

When she turned 16, Edith was sent to a Catholic boarding school. The Franciscan nuns who ran the school kept a strict schedule. Each day's activities were carefully planned. Unlike the loud, boisterous home she had come from, life at the boarding school followed a quiet routine. Meals, prayers, classes, chores, and quiet time kept to a dependable timetable. It was peaceful. From the first day she arrived Edith liked the order. She whispered to herself, "I wish this were my home."

After four months at the boarding school Edith decided to make the convent her permanent home. Like Sister Irene, who had opened the Foundling Hospital where Edith's mother had left her, Edith felt called to serve others. In 1929, the year the last orphan train ran, Edith Peterson took her vows and became a nun. Three mothers had cared for her in her life, but Edith found the home where she truly belonged among her many sisters, her fellow nuns.

Edith—now Sister Justina—found her place in life among the nuns in the Catholic order she joined in 1929.

CHAPTER EIGHT

PRETENDING TO BE HAPPY

Marguerite Driscoll Thompson

Marguerite Driscoll's unwed mother abandoned her at birth. She spent the first four years of her life in an orphanage. In 1911, at the age of five, she linked hands with two girls from the same orphanage. Together they boarded a train bound for Bertrand, Nebraska.

Marguerite was terrified. The train engine was loud. The ride was bumpy and tiring. Even worse, a train door slammed shut on her big toe. Her swollen, crushed toe made it difficult to walk. So Marguerite watched from the window as the other children got off the train at stations throughout Nebraska. Crowds of people came to look them over.

But Marguerite didn't have to line up. She had already been chosen by the Larson family. They had written to the orphanage asking for a little girl to help on their farm. She had to have been born to a Catholic mother and have dark hair and blue eyes. Marguerite fit the bill.

The Larsons came to the Bertrand train depot to claim their new daughter. Mr. Larson was a tall man with a big, bushy moustache. Marguerite could tell by the look on his face that he was kind. But she soon learned Mrs. Larson was not.

They drove Marguerite to their big home. It had two stories and ten rooms. Filled with polished furniture, it was the most beautiful place Marguerite had ever seen. The Larsons rented out three of the rooms to boarders. They kept cows and sold milk as well. A rich family, they even hired a seamstress to sew the family clothes and a laundry woman to wash them.

But as rich as they were, Mrs. Larson was very stingy. While the Larson sons slept in bedrooms, Marguerite slept on a couch in the front room. She was never allowed to use the indoor bathroom like other members of the family. Mrs. Larson claimed "it takes too much water." So Marguerite had to use the outhouse. She couldn't even bathe in the family tub. Once a week little Marguerite brought a wash tub in to the kitchen and heated water for her bath.

At the age of six she was an expert cleaner. She mopped, made beds, and scrubbed the toilet and tub she was never allowed to use.

Marguerite had no toys of her own and wasn't allowed to play with the Larson brothers' toys. When they came home from school and enjoyed a snack of bread and jam, Marguerite got none. Instead, Marguerite had to wash the dishes Mrs. Larson had left from lunch. Then she went upstairs and cleaned the boarders' bedrooms. At the age of six she was an expert cleaner. She mopped, made beds, and scrubbed the toilet and tub she was never allowed to use.

But Marguerite's workday didn't start when she came home from school. She began work before the sun came up. Rain, snow, or ice, she had to deliver heavy pails of milk to customers each morning. One dark, wintry morning Marguerite slipped on the ice. She spilled half of a customer's milk order. The angry customer phoned Mrs. Larson.

Mrs. Larson was waiting for Marguerite when she came home from school. She was holding a leather whip. "Did you drink it?" she demanded.

Trembling, Marguerite cried, "No! I slipped on the ice and it spilled."

"Liar!" yelled Mrs. Larson as she beat her. "You know you're not allowed to drink the milk." That much was true. Marguerite wasn't given a single sip of milk from the family cows. She delivered it to customers. She washed the glasses that held her brothers' milk. She helped feed the cows. But she never once tasted any of the Larsons' milk.

Her brothers could have as much as they wanted. But if Marguerite tried to eat more, Mrs. Larson said she was stealing.

She also never got enough food to eat. While the Larsons' table was filled with good things to eat, Mrs. Larson always spooned one small portion onto Marguerite's plate. Her brothers could have as much as they wanted. But if Marguerite tried to eat more, Mrs. Larson said she was stealing. Marguerite was often hungry. By the time she turned sixteen, Marguerite had lost many of her teeth due to poor nutrition.

Every year Mr. McPhealy from the Foundling Hospital came to check on Marguerite. Mrs. Larson made sure Marguerite pretended she was happy and put on a good show for him. Before each visit Marguerite had to practice a poem or song to perform for Mr. McPhealy. But Mrs. Larson couldn't stand to hear Marguerite's New York accent. As Marguerite practiced her piece, Mrs. Larson would slap her each time she sounded like a New Yorker instead of a Nebraskan.

When Mr. McPhealy arrived Marguerite recited the poem "Look on the Bright Side":

"… While through this troubled world you rove,
Be not to its attractions blind;
And if you find not much to love,
Love well the little that you find."

Afterward Marguerite danced an Irish jig for Mr. McPhealy. Then Mrs. Larson would excuse her to go outside. While the Larsons and Mr. McPhealy talked about how happy Marguerite was, Marguerite stood outside and cried. Every year she wished Mr. McPhealy would take her with him when he left. But every year she was too afraid to say anything.

When she turned 16, Marguerite gathered up her courage and ran away. She tried to join a traveling circus to escape Mrs. Larson's abuse. But Mrs. Larson had the sheriff find and return her.

Marguerite never understood why kind Mr. Larson allowed his wife to treat her so badly. Though Marguerite Driscoll never experienced a mother's love herself, she vowed that if she ever had children of her own she would be a generous, loving mother. The kind of mother she only had in her dreams.

Marguerite was treated as a servant by the Larson family.

CHAPTER NINE

A LITTLE BOY
WITH A BIG IMAGINATION

Shoppers looked for bargains. Salespeople wrapped customer's purchases. January 12, 1918, was a typical day at Gimbels, a New York department store. That is, until someone heard the baby crying. A sales clerk found the infant boy abandoned in a basket. Wearing warm, well-made clothes, he looked healthy.

The baby was given to the New York Department of Public Welfare. Because his mother couldn't be located they didn't know the boy's name or birth date.

The welfare department gave him the name Arthur Field. They had to record a birth date on his records. Arthur appeared to be around six weeks old so someone wrote down December 2, 1917, as his official birth date.

For the next few years Arthur lived with different foster families in New York. One of his earliest memories in foster care was of a Thanksgiving dinner. On that holiday he was served a plate of apple peels. There were no apples. Those had, no doubt, gone into a steaming hot Thanksgiving pie. Arthur, the foster child, just got the curled peels turning brown around the edges.

Arthur often imagined having parents of his own. No one had told him he'd been found at Gimbels. He invented stories to explain why he was an orphan.

When he was five he was sent to the Children's Aid Society. A little girl who was scheduled to ride on the next orphan train to Iowa had come down sick with the measles. The C.A.S. had already paid for twelve tickets and did not want to waste a space. They decided to send Arthur in her place.

In December 1922 Clara Comstock herded Arthur and eleven other children onto the train. "You'll like it in the west," she told Arthur. "You'll have parents of your own."

Arthur often imagined having parents of his own. No one had told him he'd been found at Gimbels. He invented stories to explain why he was an orphan. His father must have been a soldier who died in the war. His mother, Arthur decided, was a famous actress who died giving birth to him. The stories made him feel less lonely.

Along the way Miss Comstock fed the children peanut butter and jelly sandwiches and fruit from a big box. She had arranged for farmers to meet the train when it stopped at various stations. She bought fresh milk from them for the children.

As the train sped by the barren winter countryside, Miss Comstock pointed out animals to amuse the children. Arthur saw cows and horses for the first time. Miss Comstock also coached the children on how to act. "Mind your manners. Smile," she reminded them. "Don't be shy."

Arthur walked right up to Mr. Worley Smith, sat on his lap and asked, "Are you going to be my daddy?"

Arthur paid attention to Miss Comstock's lessons. He was eager to find a family. When the train arrived in Clarinda, Iowa, he followed Miss Comstock through the icy cold to the Methodist church. Inside curious farmers and their wives had packed the pews to see the orphans. Arthur walked right up to Mr. Worley Smith, sat on his lap, and asked, "Are you going to be my daddy?"

Worley and Lillian Smith had only come to the church because they were curious about the orphans. They had no intention of adopting one. But they immediately fell in love with Arthur. They took him home and raised him just like their own eight-year-old son, Cecil. In fact, Cecil and Arthur looked so much alike most people assumed they were brothers by birth.

Although Arthur had only just learned the words *cow* and *horse* from Miss Comstock, he quickly learned to help care for the family's livestock. He loved the cows, horses, pigs, and chickens. He also helped with the family's garden and strawberry patch.

Arthur (left), and his new brother, Cecil.

Best of all, he loved the food his new mother made from all the good fruits and vegetables. The smell of fresh baked bread greeted him every day after school. His new mother spread home-churned butter on the hot bread. Then she spooned her homemade strawberry jam on the top before handing Arthur the sweet, warm snack. "It was the most delicious thing in the world!"

Arthur couldn't have been happier in his new home, but sometimes his imagination acted up. He was troubled by memories of the dark Thanksgiving in foster care. He sometimes woke up in the middle of the night in a cold sweat. He screamed "Don't let them take me away from my new home." And always, he imagined his birth mother on stage singing or dancing. Lillian Smith was always there to hug him and settle him back under the covers after his bad dreams.

As an adult Arthur found out his birth father had not died in the war. His birth mother had not died in childbirth. The cold truth that she had left him in a busy department store without saying a word to anyone depressed Arthur. Once again he felt as uncared for as he had staring at that pile of Thanksgiving apple peels.

But Arthur realized he was fortunate to have good parents in Worley and Lillian Smith. Late in life he found out Lillian had even written to the Children's Aid Society. She wanted to see if they had ever found Arthur's birth mother. The C.A.S. had not found his mother. Lillian was so proud of her adopted son she had wanted to tell his birth mother about his accomplishments. When Arthur discovered this he cried. Not sad tears for the imagined mother who abandoned him. These were happy tears for the very real and caring woman who had so lovingly raised him.

CHAPTER TEN

WHAT HAPPENED TO THE RIDERS?

Some of the orphans were placed with families that treated them well, while others were treated poorly. Most of them fared better than they would have if they had been left orphaned on New York City's streets.

Two of the grown-up orphans became state governors, one became a nun, and all were able to have families of their own. Read on to find out how each rider fared as an adult.

Stanley Cornell
(CHAPTER ONE)

Stanley Cornell and his brother, Victor, remained close all their lives. Both of them served in World War II. Stanley was in the U.S. Army Signal Corps overseas. Victor enlisted in the Air Force and was stationed in Nebraska.

During the war Stanley laid telephone wire and helped keep radio and wire communications working. Stanley said in a newspaper interview that he had been the person who sent a teletype message from General Dwight D. Eisenhower announcing the war with Germany was over.

Stanley even used his communication skills to help him find his birth father, Daddy Floyd, and his sister. He sent a telegram to F.B.I. director J. Edgar Hoover asking for help. Ten days later Hoover wrote back with Daddy Floyd's address in Buffalo, New York. Eloise, who had been raised by their aunt, was now living in Cleveland, Ohio. In 1946 Stanley went to visit them.

Because he was always grateful for the good life the Degers gave him, Stanley and his wife Earleen adopted two boys of their own. After Dana and Dennis joined their family, Earleen gave birth to their daughter, Denyse.

Andrew Burke

(CHAPTER FOUR)

Burke might have remembered the advice of the boy who stood on a chair and gave a speech back at the Newsboys' Lodging to "go west, young man." As an adult Burke went very far west. He served as county treasurer for a few years. Then, the boy who hawked newspapers on New York street corners made newspaper headlines himself. He was elected governor of the new state of North Dakota in 1890.

But Andrew Burke never forgot his humble beginnings. Like the Reverend Charles Loring Brace, Burke gathered some city leaders to help the state's orphans. They established the Fargo orphan's home in 1892.

Burke later wrote to the Children's Aid Society to encourage the children there.

"Tell the boys I am proud to have had as humble a beginning in life as they, and that I believe it has been my salvation. I hope my success in life—if it can be so termed—will be an incentive to them to struggle for a respectable recognition amongst their fellow man. ... I attribute my little success in life to a few simple rules, to wit: To be honest, to be truthful, to be industrious ..., to be a student ..., to be forgiving and generous ..., and to follow the golden rule. 'Do unto others as you would have them do unto you.'"

Believe it or not, Andrew Burke wasn't the only orphan train rider to become a state governor. In fact, he wasn't even the only rider on the Noblesville, Indiana, train to become governor. His good friend John Brady was described as "the homeliest, toughest, most unpromising boy in the whole lot." Yet he was elected governor of the state of Alaska.

Agnes Ruth Anderson Hickok
(CHAPTER FIVE)

Agnes Ruth was thirteen years old when something long buried in her earliest memories turned out to be real. She had a younger sister. Miss Comstock confirmed it when she came for her yearly visit. Mrs. Jensen wrote to the Children's Aid Society to see if they could locate Agnes Ruth's birth mother or her sister. Mrs. Baxter wrote back.

"From the fact that Ruth's mother visited her in the beginning, and suddenly disappeared, it looks as if something must have happened to her, and I believe Ruth can look upon her as having died. Whatever became of Evelyn, I cannot say nor do I know any way to try to find out."

In 1931 Agnes Ruth married Orville Hickok. She continued to search for Evelyn, contacting newspapers to run the story of her search. She did hear of a woman living in Iowa who looked so much like her they could have been twins. It made her wonder if her sister, too, had ridden the orphan trains and ended up in Iowa. Ruth Hickok died in December 2003 at the age of 91 having never found her sister. Her obituary said not finding Evelyn was "a major disappointment in her life."

Robert Hunt Hume
(CHAPTER SIX)

As an adult, Robert Hunt Hume continued to be a hard worker. He farmed, learned carpentry, and did concrete work. He also became a blacksmith. His daughter, Jane, said, "If there was anything to do, he could do it!"

His dream of having a happy family came true when he married his wife, Florence. The two of them had six children of their own. They described him as a wonderful parent. In light of the way his adopted parents treated him, his daughter said "It's a miracle my dad turned out to be a nice man."

His sister Sadie worked in a telegraph office and later in an orphanage in Council Bluffs. Margaret became a teacher.

Edith Peterson
(CHAPTER SEVEN)

Edith Peterson became Sister Justina of St. Francis Convent in Little Falls, Minnesota. She made a trip to New York in 1969 to discover more about her birth parents. She found out she had three older siblings. This awakened her interest in learning more about the orphan trains. She began volunteering her time to the Orphan Train Heritage Society of America. She also attended orphan train reunions in the hope of finding her siblings.

In 1998 Sister Justina was honored with a special award. The baby left in the crib at the Foundling Hospital started by Sister Irene grew up to receive the Sister Irene award. It was given to her by the Orphan Train Heritage Society to recognize her effort to preserve the histories of the orphan train riders.

Marguerite Driscoll Thompson
(CHAPTER EIGHT)

Hard times chased Marguerite into adulthood. When her husband left her penniless after the birth of their third child, she never considered putting her children in an orphanage. Determined to be the kind of mother she never had, Marguerite took as many jobs as she could. She washed and sewed other people's clothes and cleaned houses to earn enough to feed her family.

Her daughter Jo Ann said, "We struggled. But, by golly, she kept us together. She was not about to let her kids go."

Arthur Field Smith
(CHAPTER NINE)

Arthur's imagination and ability to tell a captivating story served him well later in life. At the age of 71 he began learning more about the orphan trains. He attended orphan train reunions and began giving talks at schools about the history of the trains.

He even performed in a reenactment of an orphan train departure at the Medina, New York, Railroad Museum.

"My name is Arthur F. Smith and I put the "F" in because at one time that stood for my last name which was Field and this was the name that was given to me by the authorities in New York City when they found me."

More importantly, Arthur cared deeply about orphans and foster children. He volunteered as an advocate for children in foster care. In addition, the boy who was once a ward of the Children's Aid Society served on their board of advisors.

CHAPTER ELEVEN

WHAT HAPPENED TO THE ORPHAN TRAINS?

The Children's Aid Society sent three boys on the last orphan train to Sulfur Springs, Texas, on May 31, 1929. The Foundling Hospital had stopped its orphan train program six years earlier in 1923. For 75 years groups from three to 300 rode the rails in search of new homes. The Children's Aid Society reports having placed more than 120,000 children on orphan trains. Since other organizations sent riders as well, C.A.S. estimates the grand total of orphan train riders at 250,000. It was the largest migration of children in U.S. history. Children were sent to 48 states as well as Canada, Mexico, and England.

By some estimates one in four people in the state of Iowa have an orphan train rider in their family tree.

Today only a handful of orphan train riders are still living. But these brave children who headed west are certainly not forgotten! One organization dedicated to preserving the history of the orphan trains is the National Orphan Train Complex. They estimate 2 million people in the United States today are descendants of an orphan train rider. People living in the Midwest are the most likely to have a relative who rode the trains. That's because many riders ended up in the Midwest. By some estimates one in four people in the state of Iowa have an orphan train rider in their family tree.

One reason the trains stopped carrying children west had to do with changing state laws. Michigan was the destination of the first C.A.S. orphan train.

It was later among the states to pass a law about the placement of children within its state. The law required agencies like C.A.S. to post a bond, or deposit money, before bringing children into the state.

Near the turn of the century, Indiana, Illinois, and Minnesota all passed laws as well. These states had been frequent orphan-train destinations. Their laws made it illegal to place children they judged to be sick, mentally ill, criminal, or incorrigible. Other states followed their lead, making it difficult to transport and place children in other states.

Another reason the trains stopped running had to do with people's changing attitudes toward children as laborers. Back in the Reverend Charles Loring Brace's day, many people, including Brace, thought children ought to work to earn their keep. During the orphan-train era, there were few child labor laws. It is true that many children who rode the orphan trains found happy, loving homes. But others were simply used as labor. In fact, in many cases, the adults who took orphans in were referred to as employers, not parents.

When the Foundling Hospital placed children they were indentured. Girls were bound to their employers until the age of 18, while boys were bound until age 21. The indenture contract did state that after the age of indenture was up, the children would be treated as their legal children. That gave the children the right to inherit their parents' property. But before children came of age they might be subject to long hours of work, even abuse. The Children's Aid Society did not practice indenture. Brace thought children should be free to leave if they were unhappy.

While C.A.S. children were said to be free to leave, it wasn't always possible or the right choice. Children like Marguerite had nowhere to go. They were uprooted, separated from their siblings, placed across the country, and checked on only once a year. Runaway children were likely to face the same problems of starvation and abuse as they had before they were placed in farm homes. Still, the orphan trains served an important purpose and saved thousands of children from hardship and life on the streets.

The trains served as a kind of bridge to the modern foster care system.

Today the orphan trains are considered a step forward from the old indenture system where children could be bound for many years to an employer. The trains served as a kind of bridge to the modern foster-care system. Foster care today also seeks to place children in home settings. However, children placed in foster care are never expected to work as employees. Whenever possible, foster-care children are returned to their birth families when the parents can resume caring for them. Children in the modern foster-care system have social workers who check on them regularly. Still, like the orphan trains, it isn't a perfect system.

We can learn a lot from the stories of these brave train riders west. They were courageous, hard-working survivors.

Though the trains haven't run in close to a century, many people are still interested in them. PBS created a TV show for their American Experience series to educate people about the trains. Orphan train riders and their descendants often attend reunions, where they share stories. The National Orphan Train Complex, located in Concordia, Kansas, runs a museum and website dedicated to teaching about the trains' history. It also has resources for train riders and their families to find information about their past.

Few people are taught about the orphan trains in school. But we can learn a lot from the stories of these brave train riders west. They were courageous, hard-working survivors. Among the riders America gained two governors, a congressman, a sheriff, at least one mayor, and some district attorneys. Many grew up to be successful doctors, lawyers, bankers, teachers, farmers, ministers, and business owners. And their stories deserve to live on.

Orphan Train Timeline

1853
Charles Loring Brace founds the Children's Aid Society

1854
Newsboys' Lodging House opens

First orphan train to Dowagiac, Michigan

1859
Andrew Burke rides the train to Noblesville, Indiana

1869
Sister Irene opens the New York Foundling Hospital

1904
Robert Hunt Hume rides the train to Sidney, Iowa

1911
Marguerite Driscoll Thompson boards the train to Bertrand, Nebraska

1913
Edith Peterson arrives in Avon, Minnesota

1917
Agnes Ruth Anderson Hickok relocates to Forest City, Iowa

1922
Arthur Field Smith rides to Clarinda, Iowa

1927
Stanley Cornell finds a home in Wellington, Texas

1929
The last orphan train arrives in Sulfur Springs, Texas

Glossary

charity (CHAYR-uh-tee)—a group that raises money or collects goods to help people in need

contract (KAHN-trakt)—an agreement to do something

expedition (ek-spuh-DI-shuhn)—a group of people on a journey with a goal

immigrant (IM-uh-grunt)—someone who comes from one country to live permanently in another country

indenture (in-DEN-chur)—a contract binding one person to work for another for a certain amount of time

industrial (in-DUHSS-tree-uhl)—having to do with business and factories

institution (in-ste-TU-shen)—a place where an organization takes care of people for a long period of time

peddle (PED-uhl)—to sell something in small amounts, usually traveling from place to place

teletype (TEL-e-type)—a machine that uses a typewriter to send messages over long distances

Read More

Flanagan, Alice K. *The Orphan Trains* (We the People: Industrial America). North Mankato, Minn.: Compass Point Books, 2006.

Raum, Elizabeth. *Orphan Trains: An Interactive History Adventure.* North Mankato, Minn.: Capstone Press, 2011.

Warren, Andrea. *We Rode the Orphan Trains.* Boston: Houghton Mifflin Harcourt, 2004.

Discussion Questions

When the orphan trains began, foster parents were sometimes referred to as employers. How might that term have influenced the way some, like Mrs. Larson, treated the children they took in? (*Key Ideas and Details*)

The agreement that foster parents had to sign, agreeing to educate the children they took in, was often ignored. How might such an agreement be better enforced today? (*Integration of Knowledge and Ideas*)

If Charles Loring Brace were alive today, do you think he would have still advocated sending city children to the country for placement? Why or why not? (*Integration of Knowledge and Ideas*)

Select Bibliography

Berger, L. "Ride to Nebraska Ended in Hardship" (August 15, 2001). http://articles.latimes.com/2001/aug/15/news/cl-34282. Retrieved February 8, 2015.

Brace, C. Sequence 1 : Brace, Charles Loring. *The Best Method of Disposing of Our Pauper and Vagrant Children*[United States : S.n.], 1859. Harvard University Library PDS. http://pds.lib.harvard.edu/pds/view/3290622. Retrieved February 9, 2015.

Brace, C. *The Dangerous Classes of New York and Twenty Years' Work Among Them.* http://www.gutenberg.org/cache/epub/33431/pg33431.html. Retrieved February 9, 2015.

Connor, S. Orphan trains: The Story of Charles Loring Brace and the Children He Saved and Failed (2001). Boston: Houghton Mifflin.

De la Cueva, L. "Our hip, cool nun," *Minnesota Women's Press.* http://www.womenspress.com/print.asp?ArticleID=3185&SectionID=1&SubSectionID=1. Retrieved February 11, 2015.

Dush, B. "Families of Orphan Train riders keep history alive, TheFencePost.com (April 8, 2010). http://www.thefencepost.com/article/20100411/NEWS/100409938. Retrieved February 12, 2015.

Frese, M. (Ed.). "Ruth Hickok," 2000. Goldfinch: Iowa History for Young People, 21(3).

Iowa GenWeb Project Welcome Page Orphan Train Riders to Iowa Webster County. http://iagenweb.org/. Retrieved February 12, 2015.

Jackson, D. "Trains Ferried Waifs To New Lives On The Prairie" (September 28, 1986). http://articles.sun-sentinel.com/1986-09-28/features/8602270532_1_charles-loring-brace-orphan-trains-noah-lawyer/2. Retrieved February 8, 2015.

McShane, G. "Woman Hopes to Reunite with Sister" (August 1, 1988). Retrieved http://newspaperarchive.com/us/minnesota/albert-lea-tribune/1988/08-14/. February 8, 2015.

Mitchell, K. (Pueblo County Biographies Stanley Cornell. http://www.kmitch.com/Pueblo/bios0052.html. Retrieved February 11, 2015.

Orphan Train Riders Agents. http://iagenweb.org/history/orphans/agents/Comstock_C.htm. Retrieved January 25, 2015.

Patrick, M., and E. Trickel. Orphan Trains to Missouri. Columbia: University of Missouri Press, 1997.

Roberts, J. "Remembering the Trains that Brought Orphans West," (April 19, 2004). http://news.wbfo.org/post/remembering-trains-brought-orphans-west. Retrieved March 15, 2015.

Siegal, N. (2000, May 12). "Riders of 'Orphan Train' Meet to Tell Life Stories," (May 12, 2000). http://www.nytimes.com/2000/05/13/nyregion/riders-of-orphan-train-meet-to-tell-life-stories.html. Retrieved February 8, 2015.

Thompson, M. "Marguerite Thompson http://orphantraindepot.org/orphan-train-rider-stories/marguerite-thompson. ." Retrieved January 25, 2015.

Torigoe, J. "Orphan Train Rider Stanley Cornell," (December 24, 2008). http://www.cnn.com/2008/LIVING/wayoflife/12/24/orphan.trains/index.html?erer_opinion. Retrieved January 26, 2015.

Vossler, B. North Dakota Horizons -- Horizons Magazine. http://www.ndhorizons.com/featured/index.asp?ID=69. Retrieved January 26, 2015.

Warren, A. We Rode the Orphan Trains. Boston: Houghton Mifflin, 2001.

Source Notes

page 43, "Boys, (gentlemen), chummies: (Perhaps)…" Brace, C. The Dangerous Classes of New York and Twenty Years' Work Among Them. http://www.gutenberg.org/cache/epub/33431/pg33431.html. (Retrieved February 9, 2015)

pages 44–45, "Yesterday afternoon Mr. C. C. Tracy left this city for the West, with another company of little ones from the Children's Aid…" Juvenile Emigration Newspapers.com - Historical Newspapers from 1700s-2000s. (May 18, 1859). http://www.newspapers.com. Retrieved February 2, 2015.

page 46, "It was the most motley crowd of youngsters I ever did see." O'Connor, page 180.

page 46, "I decided to take John Brady home with me…" O'Connor, p 180.

page 50, "Don't touch me," Mama said. "I'm sick." Warren, A. (1998, November 1). The Orphan Train. http://www.washingtonpost.com/wpsrv/national/horizon/nov98/orphan.htm. Retrieved February 8, 2015.

page 53, "Don't worry," another orphan told her. "They landed." Frese, M. (Ed.). (2000). Ruth Hickok. *Goldfinch: Iowa History for Young People, 21*(3).

page 53, "See?" he said. "The seeds inside the apple will grow apple trees next to the train tracks," Warren, p. 57.

page 54, "If you don't stop that crying you'll get no supper," Warren, p. 59.

page 56, "This isn't going to work out," Warren, p. 60.

page 57, "I don't want to sleep in a cellar where it's black and smelly!" Frese.

page 57, "Is it all mine?" Agnes asked, Warren, p. 60.

page 64, "I'll give you back the bracelet and the candy if you give me back my sister" Dush, B. "Families of Orphan Train riders keep history alive," TheFencePost.com (April 8, 2010) http://www. thefencepost.com/article/20100411/NEWS/100409938. Retrieved February 12, 2015.

pages 66–67, "I, the undersigned _____ hereby agree to…" Ancestry.com

page 78, "I wish this were my home," De la Cueva, L. "Our hip, cool nun," Minnesota Women's Press, http://www.womenspress. com/print.asp?ArticleID=3185&SectionID=1&SubSection ID=1. Retrieved February 11, 2015.

page 84, "Did you drink it? she demanded," Riley, T. The Orphan Trains. http://irishamerica.com/2014/03the-orphan-trains/. Retrieved February 8, 2015.

page 86, "Look on the Bright Side," poem by John Bowring.

page 91, "You'll like it in the west," Warren, p. 67.

page 92, "Mind your manners." Warren, A. (2001). *We Rode the Orphan Trains*. Boston: Houghton Mifflin. p. 68.

page 92, "Are you going to be my daddy?" Siegal, N. "Riders of 'Orphan Train' Meet to Tell Life Stories" *New York Times* (May 13, 2000). http://www.nytimes.com/2000/05/13/ nyregion/riders-of-orphan-train-meet=-to-tell-life-stories.html. Retrieved February 8, 2015.

page 94, "Don't let them take me away from my new home…" Warren, p. 70.

pages 100–101, "Tell the boys I am proud to have had as humble a beginning in life as they, and that I believe it has been my…" Vossler, B. http://www.ndhorizons.com/featured/index.asp?ID=69. Retrieved January 26, 2015.

page 102, "From the fact that Ruth's mother visited her in the beginning, and suddenly disappeared, it…" McShane, G. "Woman Hopes to Reunite with Sister" (August 1, 1988). http://newspaperarchive.com/us/minnesota/albert-lea-tribune/1988/08-14/. Retrieved February 8, 2015.

page 103, Her obituary said not finding Evelyn was "a major disappointment in her life." www.pafways.info/forestcitysummit/2003/december.htm

page 104, "If there was anything to do, he could do it…" Dush, B. "Families of Orphan Train Riders Keep History Alive, TheFencePost.com (April 8, 2010). http://www.thefencepost.com/article/20100411/NEWS/100409938, Retrieved February 12, 2015.

page 104, "It's a miracle my dad turned out…" Dush.

page 106, Her daughter Jo Ann said, "We struggled. But, by golly,…" Berger, L. "Ride to Nebraska Ended in Hardship" (August 15, 2001). http://articles.latimes.com/2001/aug/15/news/cl-34282. Retrieved February 8, 2015.

page 107, "My name is Arthur F. Smith and I put the "F" in because…" Roberts, J. Remembering the Trains that Brought Orphans West. http://news.wbfo.org/post/remembering-trains-brought-orphans-west. Retrieved March 15, 2015.

Index

Rebecca Langston-George is an elementary school teacher in California's central valley. Her previous books include *For the Right to Learn: Malala Yousafzai's Story, Telling Tales: Writing Captivating Short Stories,* and *A Primary Source History of the Dust Bowl.* Rebecca serves as the Assistant Regional Advisor for the Central-Coastal chapter of the Society of Children's Book Writers and Illustrators. You can read more about the author at *www.rebeccalangston-george.com.*